AF658727

REMARKABLE WILDLIFE

JOHN LESLEY

LION

REDBACK publishing

First Published 2026 by
Redback Publishing
Suite 6, 13a Narabang Way,
Belrose NSW 2085
Australia

www.redbackpublishing.com
orders@redbackpublishing.com

© Redback Publishing 2026

ISBN 978-1-761402-02-9

All rights reserved. No part of this publication may be reproduced in any form or by any means (including photocopying or storing it in any medium by electronic means and whether or not transiently or incidentally to some other use of this publication) without the written permission of the copyright owner. Applications for the copyright owner's written permission should be addressed to the publisher.

Author: John Lesley
Editor: Lucinda Dodds and Emma Dobinson
Designer: Redback Publishing

Original illustrations © Redback Publishing 2026
Originated by Redback Publishing

Acknowledgements
Abbreviations: l—left, r—right, b—bottom, t—top, c—centre, m—middle
We would like to thank the following for permission to reproduce photographs (images © Shutterstock unless otherwise stated) p18-19m W. Gornig, CC BY-SA 4.0 <https://creativecommons.org/licenses/by-sa/4.0>, via Wikimedia Commons, p19bl Jose manuel canete, CC BY-SA 4.0 <https://creativecommons.org/licenses/by-sa/4.0>, via Wikimedia Commons

MIX
Paper from responsible sources
FSC™ C001507

Disclaimer
Every effort has been made to contact copyright holders of any material reproduced in this book.
Any omissions will be rectified in subsequent printings if notice is given to the publisher.

A catalogue record for this book is available from the National Library of Australia

CONTENTS

WHAT IS A LION?

Lions are 'big cats', a term that refers to just five types of large cats. Lions are the second largest cats in the world, after the tiger, which is the longest and heaviest big cat.

Feared predator, circus performer, symbol of strength and of family, the lion has been used to represent many aspects of human life for many thousands of years.

The true nature of the mighty lion has often been lost in the symbolism. Lions are not as strong and all-powerful as we might think. Currently under threat in its natural habitats, the lion could easily become extinct in the near future.

KING OF THE JUNGLE?

No, not really. Lions live and hunt on savannahs, which are grasslands that are sparsely wooded. They do not live in jungles.

Q: Are mountain lions the same as other lions?

A: No, they are a different kind of big cat.

Mountain lion

LION BASIC FACTS

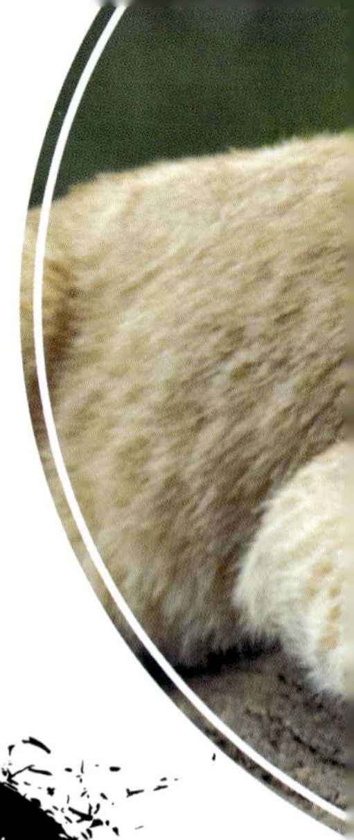

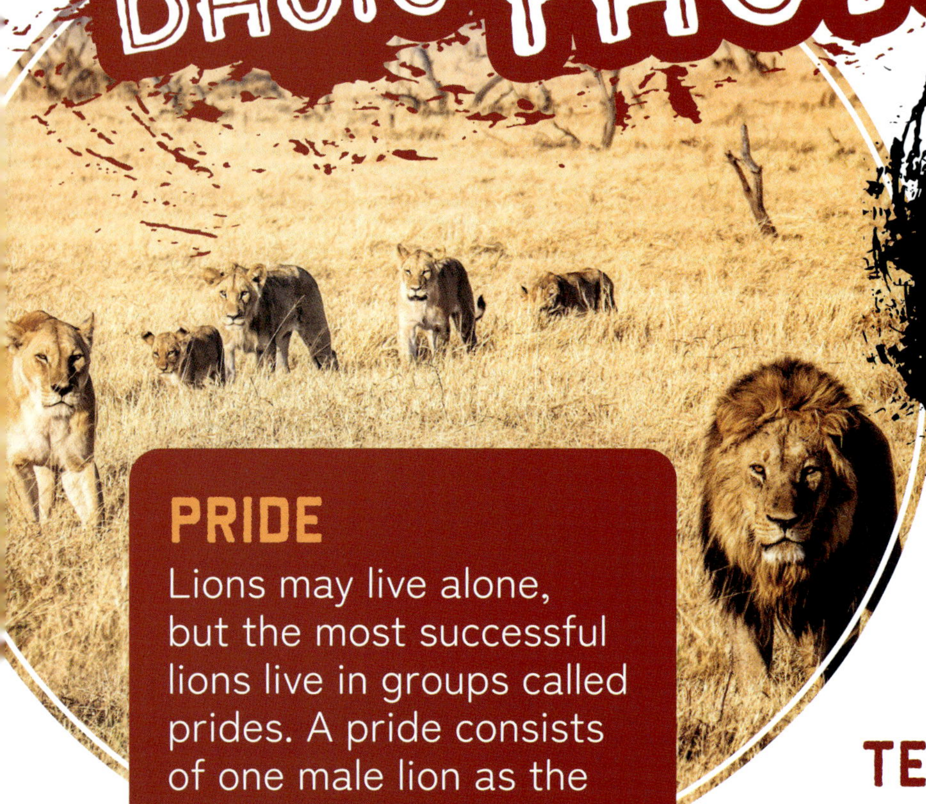

SIZE

Male lions are bigger than females. They grow to over a metre high and the body can be two metres long.

PRIDE

Lions may live alone, but the most successful lions live in groups called prides. A pride consists of one male lion as the leader, plus females, cubs and a few younger males. The pride hunts together, shares its food and protects its members. Some lions in a pride keep watch so that others can sleep in safety during the day, and all the cubs gather in a group that is looked after by one or two females.

TEETH AND CLAWS

Lions have a bite that can easily crush bones. They kill large prey by biting the throat and holding on so that the animal cannot breathe.

Lion claws are long and strong. They use them to grab prey and pull it down so that they can reach the neck and bite it. Lions also use their claws for defence and to help them climb onto the lower branches of trees.

ROARING

The ability to roar is a characteristic that places a lion in the genus called *Panthera*. Other cats that cannot roar, such as cheetahs and even domestic cats, are not classed as big cats. Lions have a special bone in their throat that allows them to make this deep and loud noise.

Lions use their mighty roar to communicate. The sound can be heard far away, letting other lions know that a particular territory has already been taken and that they should keep away.

COLOUR

Lions are covered in fur that ranges in colour from sandy yellow to brown. Cubs have pale spots that help to camouflage them in the long, dry grass when they are hiding. Adult lions develop a black tuft at the tip of the tail.

KG

WEIGHT

An adult male lion weighs around 200 kilograms.

LION ADAPTATIONS

Lions can see well at night and in the day, so they can hunt at any time.

RUNNING

Lions can run extremely fast for a short distance, but they quickly lose energy if the prey animal is a fast runner and manages to escape. The lion then stops the chase and turn its attention to a slower animal.

CLAWS

Retractable claws let lions run fast on the pads of their feet.

HUNTING

Lions are perfectly adapted to living on open grasslands where there are animals for them to hunt. They have evolved to work together to bring down even very large animals, such as a giraffe. The group of lions circles the prey, leaving it no way to escape. Some of the lions then grab the animal's hind legs or rump with their claws, while others attack the neck and try to stop the animal breathing.

STRENGTH IN NUMBERS

Living in a pride is a social adaptation that provides lions with food, grooming and baby-sitting for the cubs. There is no other animal on the African savannah that could succeed in killing a lion that was protected by the pride.

COMMUNICATING

Lions are very intelligent. As with all intelligent animals, they do a lot of communicating with each other. They make many different sounds, ranging from a roar to a purr. Male lions also use smell to let other lions know that they are in charge. Just like a domestic cat, lions spray urine around their territory. When another lion smells this they know exactly what the smell means.

LION HABITAT

As lions move out of natural habitats, they come into conflict with local villagers and farmers.

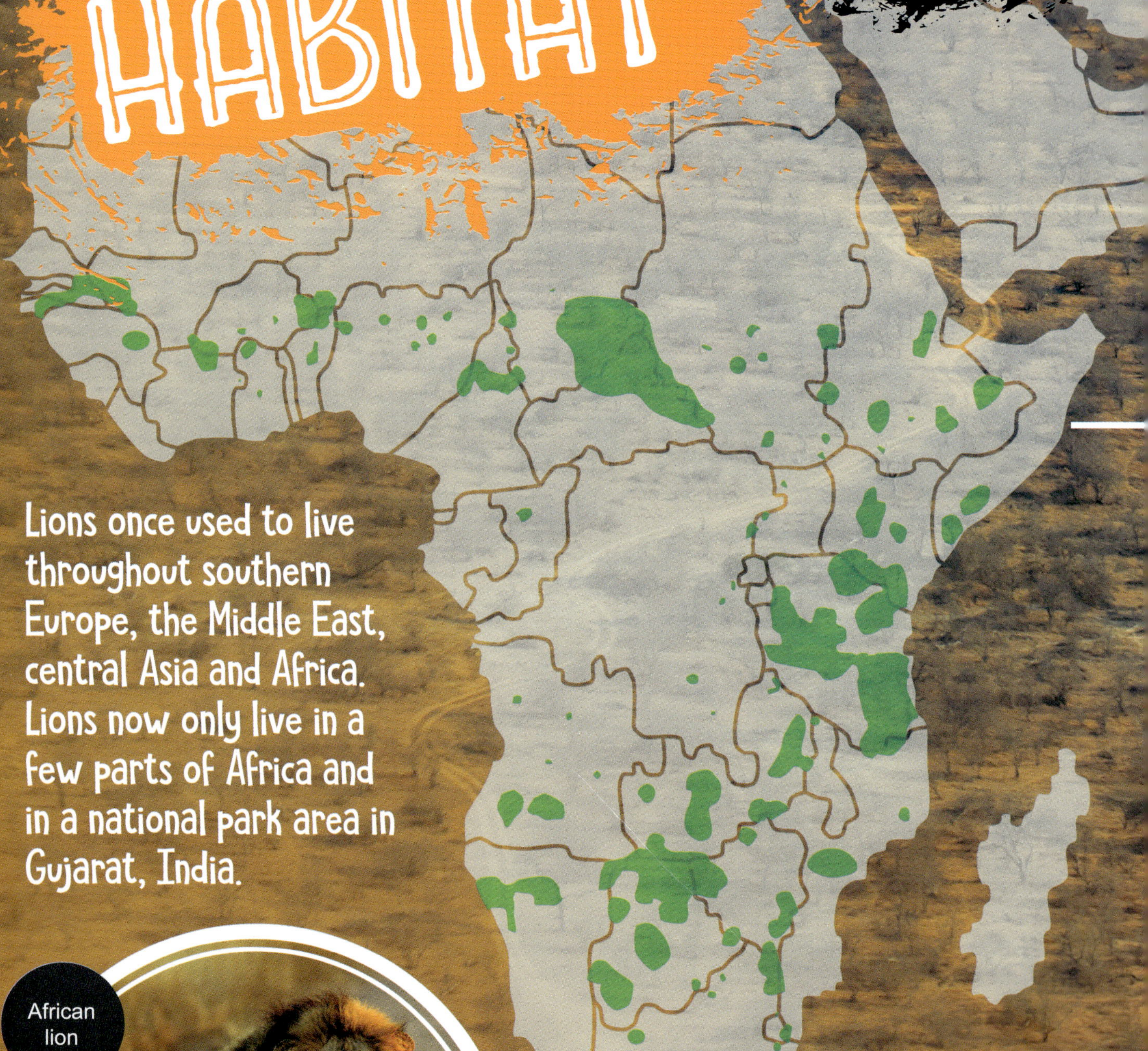

Lions once used to live throughout southern Europe, the Middle East, central Asia and Africa. Lions now only live in a few parts of Africa and in a national park area in Gujarat, India.

African lion

THESE TWO GROUPS OF LIONS ARE SEPARATE SUBSPECIES:

Panthera leo leo (Africa)
Panthera leo persica (India)

INDIA

The lions in India are called Asiatic lions. They are confined to the Gir Forest in India, a small area where they are protected. Asiatic lions do not have a wide savannah to hunt in. Instead, they live and hunt in open forest and scrub.

AFRICA

African lions live in the savannah regions, which are large areas of grasslands with few trees. This is also the habitat of the lion's main prey animals. Lions have evolved to stalk their prey by hiding in the long, dry grass, then attacking as a group so that the animal does not escape. Lions drink at waterholes that they sometimes share with their prey animals.

Most of the African lions are in the game parks. Any that wander beyond the park borders are likely to be killed by people.

Asiatic lion

The Indian lion is smaller than the African lion, and the male has a darker-coloured mane.

LION LIFE CYCLE

BIRTH

The lion life cycle starts when a male and female mate. The female lion gives birth to one or two lion cubs and feeds them on milk. The spotted, newborn cubs are completely helpless and depend on their mother for everything. She hides them in long grass where they know to stay still and quiet when she goes away to hunt for food.

JOINING THE PRIDE

When the cubs have grown bigger, the lionesses introduce them to the rest of the pride. This can be a dangerous time for the cubs, as the head male lion needs to accept them. If he does not, then he will kill the cubs.

Lion cubs stay with their mothers for about two years, learning everything they need to know to become skilled hunters and protectors.

LEAVING THE PRIDE

If all goes well, the cubs grow up surrounded by the protection of the pride. As they get older, male cubs are driven away and tend to form small groups with other young males. Female juveniles may also leave and may try to join another pride, or to start a new one. The availability of a territory that has not been taken by another pride restricts the formation of too many new prides.

LIFESPAN

Lions can live for 10 to 15 years in the wild, but up to 20 years in a zoo. Male lions usually live shorter lives. They can be injured in fights for territory, or protecting the pride from attacks. All lions are prone to getting infections and arthritis as they age. which means that they cannot hunt easily and may become too weak to survive.

WHAT LIONS EAT

CARNIVORES

Lions are carnivores and are not known to eat any plants at all. Adult lions in Africa prey on large animals. These include wildebeest, zebra, gazelles and young elephants. In India, lions take deer, antelope and wild buffalo.

HUNTING

Adult lions prefer to hunt large animals that can be quickly killed. Some lions hunt alone, but they are more successful when they hunt as a group. Lions may eat as soon as the kill is made, or they sometimes drag the kill to a safe area and hide it from other predators that could try to steal it.

WATCH OUT

A lion can become a man-eater, sometimes attacking people in fields and villages. Livestock are also at risk. Farmers living along the borders of national parks where lions roam often report lions killing their animals. Lions may also scavenge from other predators, such as hyenas, feeding on prey that has already been killed.

YOUNG LIONS

Young lions practise their hunting skills by stalking small animals such as birds and lizards. An adult lion may also do this, but bringing down a large animal with a lot of meat on it is a better result. A large kill is more useful as it will also feed the cubs and the rest of the pride. Lions prefer to feed only every few days, when they eat a lot of meat all at once.

HEALTHY HERDS

The presence of lions has a positive effect on the whole environment. Lions prefer to prey on slower and sick animals, which improves the overall fitness of the herd.

APEX PREDATORS

GRAZING ANIMALS

ENVIRONMENT

The presence of apex predators in a biome is one of nature's ways of stopping any one group of animals increasing in numbers and damaging the whole ecosystem.

Lions are apex predators. This means that a strong, healthy adult does not have to fear any other animal.

Because grazing animals are a lion's main prey, keeping the herd numbers under control is an important way that lions contribute to grasslands not being overgrazed.

An environment can quickly become unbalanced if anything in the habitat changes. For example, climate change that results in less rainfall and therefore less grass will affect the numbers and health of both the grazing animals and the lions who depend on them for survival.

Humans are the main threats to lions.

WHERE DID LIONS COME FROM?

Lions have been on Earth for millions of years, which is long before humans evolved. There were once many more species of lions, but they all became extinct, leaving only the African and Indian lions alive today.

The ancient lions on Earth were large and fierce. Here are just two whose fossils have been found:

SABRE-TOOTHED LIONS

Smilodon was a type of ancient lion that existed from two million years ago right up until the end of the last Ice Age, about 10,000 years ago. Commonly called the sabre-toothed lion, some of them weighed over 400 kilograms. They get their name from their sword-like, canine teeth. *Smilodon* is sometimes called a sabre-toothed tiger, but it was not closely related to tigers at all. It lived in the Americas, where it would have killed and been killed by ancient human hunters.

CAVE LION

The cave lion of Europe and America, *Panthera spelaea*, became extinct about 10,000 years ago. It was one of the largest lions that has ever lived, with a body that was over two metres long.

MARSUPIAL LIONS

The marsupial lion, *Thylacoleo carnifex*, that used to live in Australia about two million years ago, was not related to modern lions. It was a marsupial, which means that it carried its babies in a pouch, just like modern marsupials do.

LIONS AND PEOPLE

In Africa and India, where the only remaining wild lions live, protected areas are bordered with farms and villages. If lions cross these borders they are likely to be killed because of the danger they pose to both people and their livestock.

African nature reserves are attempting to conserve lions by providing tourist encounters instead of hunting trips. Tourists can get close to lions by driving through the reserve. They can also spend time in tourist resorts that allow them to see the wild animals in their natural surroundings.

CIRCUSES

In many parts of the world, using lions in circuses is now considered an unacceptable way to treat them.

Poaching is the illegal taking and killing of animals. In the game reserves of Africa, poaching of lions is one of the problems that conservation officers have to deal with. Lion skins and body parts can sell for large amounts of money on the black market.

BLACK MARKET

The black market refers to the illegal trade in animals and their body parts.

LIONS IN ZOOS

Lions have been kept in zoos for thousands of years. The ancient Romans even used them in violent contests with gladiators to see who would win!

In modern zoos, lions are treated as ambassadors for their species. When we see a lion pride at a zoo, it is easier for us to understand how important it is for lions to be protected from extinction.

Wild lions have large territories covering many square kilometres. Keeping zoo lions in the largest enclosure possible allows people to see more of their natural behaviour.

Some zoos allow lion cubs to be cuddled and patted by human visitors. This is a thrilling experience for people, who would never be able to touch a lion in any other setting.

In some places, lions are still kept in small cages.

LIONS AS SYMBOLS

Lions have been used in art since people began drawing them on cave walls across Europe thousands of years ago. Since then, lions have become symbols of bravery and strength.

The coat of arms of the United Kingdom has a lion on it representing the nation. The State Emblem of India shows three lions together.

In China, where lions are not known to have existed in the wild, statues of guardian lions bring good luck and protection.

Lions became a symbol of royalty and courage across all of the areas where they used to roam in Europe, Asia and Africa.

THE LION, THE WITCH AND THE WARDROBE

In recent times, lions have been used as characters in novels, cartoons, movies and plays. The famous series of stories by C.S. Lewis, *The Lion, the Witch and the Wardrobe*, portrays the lion, Aslan, as a symbol of religion and power.

LEO

Leo the lion is one of the twelve astrological signs of the western zodiac.

ENDANGERED LIONS

In India there may be only about 500 lions left in the wild.

We are so used to seeing lions in wildlife documentaries, in zoos and represented in books and movies, that it is easy to form the impression that they must be very safe from extinction. Sadly, this is not the case.

There may be only 25,000 wild lions left in Africa.

Lions are under threat in both Africa and India, the only two places in the world where they still exist in the wild. The main threat to their continued existence comes from the loss of their natural habitat. Humans are increasing in population around the world, and we need more room for farms, houses and towns. This puts a strain on the wildlife that lives in all the areas that were once covered in forests and grassland.

RED LIST

The International Union for Conservation of Nature (IUCN) Red List is a catalogue of living things and their state of conservation. African lions are now listed as being Vulnerable. Asiatic lions are listed as Endangered.

OTHER BIG CATS

Lions are one of the five big cats in the genus group called Panthera: tiger, lion, jaguar, leopard, snow leopard.

Snow leopard

Tiger

Jaguar

Panther (Leopard)

A panther is a black jaguar or leopard.

All cats, big and small, are classed in the family *Felidae*. That means your pet cat is related to a lion!

Lynx

While people often call them 'wild cats', species like the cougar, cheetah, ocelot, and lynx are not classified as true big cats.

Ocelot

Cougar (Mountain lion, Puma)

Cheetah

SORTING ANIMALS INTO GROUPS

Biologists divide all living things around the world into groups. They call this process classification.

ANIMALS ARE CLASSIFIED INTO TWO MAIN GROUPS:

VERTEBRATES

Vertebrates have a backbone

INVERTEBRATES

Invertebrates do not have a backbone

Vertebrates are further divided into five groups called classes:

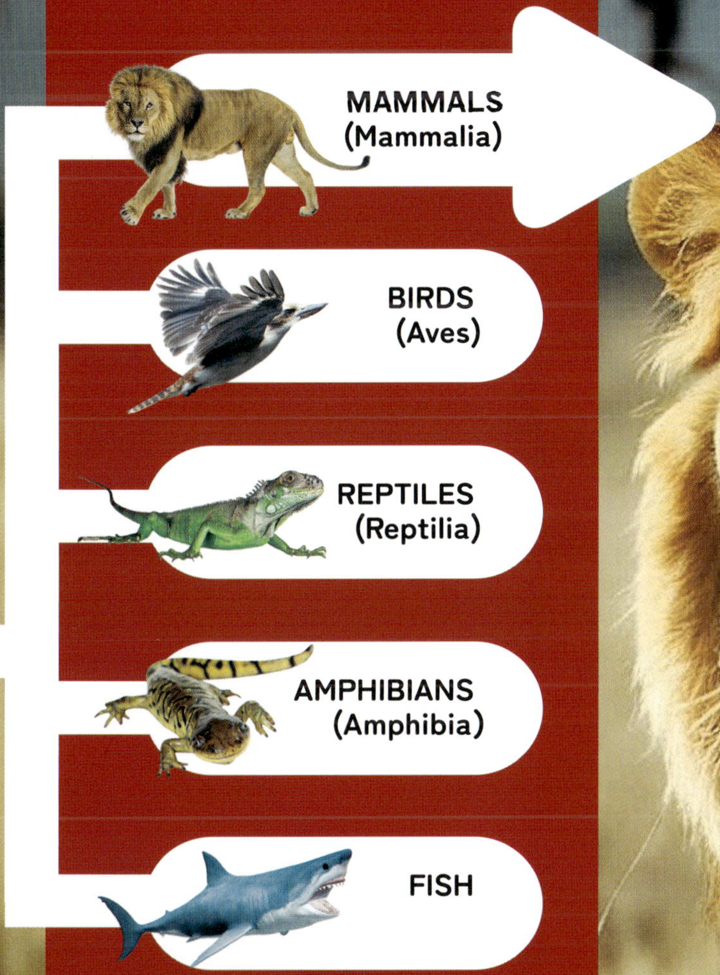

Humans are in the class called Mammalia. Lions are mammals and also belong in the class called Mammalia.

GLOSSARY

apex predator	strongest hunter in a biome
black market	illegal trade in animals and their body parts
camouflage	disguise appearance as a way of hiding
carnivore	meat eater
genus	scientific name for groupings of living things
poaching	illegally taking animals from the wild
predator	animal that hunts another for food
prey *(noun)*	animals hunted for food
retractable	able to be drawn back
savannah	grassland with few trees
scavenge	eat food or dead animals left by other animals
stalk	hunt quietly and silently
territory	area that an animal claims for itself

INDEX